Original title:
Love Rekindled

Copyright © 2024 Creative Arts Management OÜ
All rights reserved.

Author: Natalie Green
ISBN HARDBACK: 978-9908-0-1302-2
ISBN PAPERBACK: 978-9908-0-1303-9

Raindrops on the Windowpane

Raindrops tap a silly beat,
We dance in puddles, oh so sweet.
Your socks are soggy, what a mess!
But who needs dry when we can jest?

Umbrellas flipped, we're laughing loud,
A clown parade, we make a crowd.
You slip on mud, a graceful fall,
And still we giggle through it all.

Serenade of Old Affections

We sing the songs of yesteryear,
Your off-key notes bring me such cheer.
My heart does a tango, it seems absurd,
As you butcher every single word.

Your dancing style? A floppy seal,
Yet I cheer you on with squeals of zeal.
Once shy, now bold, our antics thrive,
With every move, we feel alive!

Through the Lens of Time

Old photos show our awkward poses,
You with a fro, like blooming roses.
I wore that shirt, so very bright,
A fashion crime, but oh, what a sight!

We laugh at styles from days gone by,
Your 'cool' sunglasses, a butterfly.
Through time we glide, like silly sprites,
With goofy smiles in all our bites.

When Hearts Remember

You stole my fries; I stole a kiss,
In our silly world, how could we miss?
You crack a joke to break the ice,
Our goofy banter is oh so nice.

Like two old socks that found their mate,
Our quirks together, oh, what a fate!
With every smile, the sparks ignite,
We juggle laughter, morning till night.

The Reunion of Forgotten Dreams

We met again, oh what a sight,
Your goofy grin brought pure delight.
The nights we spent in that old cafe,
Laughing at jokes, come what may.

Remember those times we were so bold,
Dancing like toddlers, feeling quite old.
You still can't keep a straight face, I see,
That charm of yours still tickles me.

We found our way through paths unplanned,
Stumbling and fumbling, hand in hand.
Now ice cream fights turn to sweet embraces,
With you, my heart just races.

So here we are, a quirky pair,
Replaying moments beyond compare.
With every giggle that slips our lips,
We toast to life's funny little trips.

Unfurling Again

Oh, look who's back with that crazy hat,
Trying to charm like a sleek, cool cat.
You tell the same jokes, but I still laugh,
Your rhythm's like an old photograph.

Remember the time you tripped on a shoe?
You fell, but pulled me, so I went too.
We rolled on the grass, laughing out loud,
Sharing the secrets that made us proud.

Now we stumble on memories, sweet and bright,
Finding our steps in the soft moonlight.
Your hand finds mine, it's a perfect fit,
A waltz of bemusement, what a hit!

And here we are, letting dreams collide,
In this silly dance, there's no need to hide.
With every chuckle, we build up the fire,
Our hearts play the tunes of pure desire.

The Sweetness of Rediscovery

You walked in like a candy store,
I surely can't resist anymore.
With every glance, my heart skips by,
Did you get funnier, or am I shy?

The pranks we played in long-lost days,
Seem more like mischief in quirky ways.
Chasing you down for a piece of cake,
The sweet little mess that we both make.

Now we chuckle over coffee cups,
Sharing the bubbly, and hiccupping ups.
We've turned the mundane into delight,
Like silly kids, we own the night.

Old souvenirs dance in my mind,
Each memory, more precious, entwined.
Hands in pockets, we stroll with glee,
Rediscovering us, just you and me.

A Canvas of Us

We grab the brushes, colors in hand,
Mixing our pasts as we make our stand.
Each stroke a giggle, splashes of fun,
A masterpiece formed by two, not one.

Your wild strokes swirl, they twist and play,
And I can't help but take your paint away.
We dance around canvases, no fear in sight,
Creating our stories, oh what a sight!

The canvas brightens, with laughter and glee,
Every silly mishap sets our hearts free.
Who knew that art was a joke we shared?
In this whirlwind of color, we're both ensnared.

So here's to the palette of you and me,
A whimsical journey, just let it be.
In this gallery of joy, we forever roam,
Painting the picture that feels like home.

When Time Paused for Us

In a coffee shop we met again,
You spilled your drink, yet I felt no pain.
We laughed so hard, the barista grinned,
As memories flowed, our stories pinned.

You wore those socks with holes, oh dear!
I tried to hide my laughter, sincere.
We danced like fools to that old jukebox,
Turns out our hearts outmatched the clocks.

Flowers in the Attic

We found a box of old love notes,
Covered in dust, like long-lost goats.
You read aloud, I rolled my eyes,
Each word was sweet, a funny surprise.

There were doodles, hearts and silly lines,
A secret garden that still shines.
We laughed at how we used to swoon,
Now we argue over who gets the moon.

When Shadows Melt Away

In the park, we reminisce at dusk,
Your jokes still hit like fragrant musk.
We chased our shadows, giggling loud,
Once lost in clouds, now we're so proud.

You tripped on grass, and I could not breathe,
Our laughter echoed, a sweet reprieve.
When shadows fade, it's pure delight,
Old sparks flicker in the fading light.

Threads of Connection

Worn-out sweaters, threads all frayed,
Just like our hearts, but still unscathed.
You knit a joke in every purl,
I laugh so hard, around we twirl.

Your cooking skills? A culinary crime!
Yet I devour it each single time.
With every bite, we share our dreams,
Life's a comedy, or so it seems.

A Sea of Familiarity

In the kitchen, we bickering,
You stole my last slice, it's irritating!
But the smile on your face, a tease I adore,
Together we laugh, who could ask for more?

Old jokes resurface, like a great old wine,
Each punchline lands, with timing divine.
We dance through the mess, like a comic routine,
Amidst flour and sugar, you're my favorite scene.

Rechasing the Stars

We once dreamed of the moon, on a late-night drive,
But the car broke down, nearly sent me to hide.
We laughed at the mishap, under the streetlight,
Like stars in the sky, we shone oh so bright.

Writing our wishes on a fast food receipt,
Just you and the fries, this adventure's a treat!
With ketchup packets, we plan our escape,
To conquer the universe, a giggling landscape.

Paths Intertwined Again

We took separate routes, like wayward socks,
But somehow found each other, like mismatched clocks.
Your quirky charm, it pulls me right back,
Together we stroll down that familiar track.

Let's trip over memories, laugh at our past,
Feeding each other, popcorn to last.
Who knew that a movie, with you on my side,
Would make all the chaos feel like a ride?

Moments on Repeat

Like a record that skips, we found the right groove,
Bumping into old highs, as we start to move.
With each silly smile, another chuckle arises,
Like discovering new snacks, in old surprising sizes.

We stumble through life, as if on a stage,
The audience laughing, we flip every page.
With inside jokes, and silly handshakes,
The rerun of us, is what love truly makes.

Embers of Yesterday

In a cozy nook, we share our pies,
Your hand slips, and I hear the sighs.
Remember the dance that knocked over the chair?
You tried to impress, but we laughed at the air.

In comfy slippers, we chase the cat,
Your joke falls flat—it's more like a splat.
Yet, the spark in your eye shines bright like a star,
Silly moments with you are the best by far.

Echoes in the Heart

We argue over movies, who likes which part,
You swear you're a genius, but I've got the chart.
Yet as we bicker, I still steal a glance,
Your goofy expressions give me a chance.

In the kitchen chaos, we make quite a team,
Burnt toast is the prize from our breakfast dream.
I'll take the syrup, you'll want the hash,
Even with a mix-up, our giggles still clash.

Streets Where We Once Danced

On cobblestone paths where we twirled and spun,
A squirrel darted by—it's always so fun.
You tripped on your shoe, oh dear, what a sight!
We laughed 'til we cried under soft city lights.

With ice cream in hand, we raced to the split,
You dropped yours on the ground, and now you just sit.
But the sweetness remains, like a cherry on top,
We chase after moments, never wanting to stop.

Whispers of Old Promises

In the attic of dreams, we rummage around,
Finding treasures and trinkets, old love letters found.
They're filled with the quirks of how you adore,
Reminding me daily what we're both here for.

We sit on the floor, sharing wine from a cup,
You toast to my quirks, and I say, "What's up?"
Old promises linger like sweet perfume,
In this goofy ballet of our silly love bloom.

Rediscovering Hidden Paths

We stumbled on that old café,
Where we once danced, just to sway.
Your coffee spill, my pastry tease,
Stirring up memories with such ease.

The jukebox played our favorite tune,
We both laughed, like a couple of loons.
You stole my fries, I rolled my eyes,
Yet deep inside, I felt the rise.

As we roamed the streets, hand in hand,
We got lost, but it was well planned.
A detour here, a trip down the lane,
Rebooting laughter, dodging the mundane.

Who knew a drive would make us smile,
Counting squirrels as we went the extra mile?
Your silly faces, my goofy song,
In this quirky world, we both belong.

Flickers in the Ashes

Remember the time we burnt the toast?
You laughed, I grumbled, called for a host.
Flames flickered, but so did our humor,
Crispy edges made us a bit of a rumor.

The fireplace crackled, the shadows danced,
You whispered secrets, I was entranced.
In smoke and giggles, we stoked the fire,
Every chuckle raised our spirits higher.

We rekindled spark, like an old camp flame,
Every burnt bagel, never the same.
Your snorts of laughter, my playful pout,
In the chaos, there's no doubt.

With each charred bite, we toasted the night,
Finding joy in flaws, everything felt right.
Two goofballs together, through thick and thin,
In the embers of life, we found the win.

Avoiding the Inevitable Goodbye

It's the last call, but we stay so late,
Pretending to linger, oh isn't it great?
Your eye twinkle says 'not now',
But time's a thief, oh, take a bow!

We dodge the clock, like it's a game,
Silly banter, but it's not the same.
Each tick is a tease, we laugh and we sigh,
Using up our minutes, as moments fly by.

We chat of wild dreams, lost in our schemes,
Delaying the end—oh, what a team!
But one last hug, like a sticky gum,
Pulling away, we know it's done.

Yet here we are, doing the dance,
The "you leave first" and "give it a chance."
With every embrace, we tease and we sway,
It's harder to part, but we find a way.

Reflections in a Loving Mirror

We look in the mirror, and what do we see?
Two silly faces, laughing with glee.
Your bedhead is wild, mine's sadly the same,
In this fun house of love, it feels like a game.

We see our quirks, the odd little traits,
You dance like no one, I muffle the grates.
With every glance, a giggle ensues,
In this funhouse of colors, there's always a muse.

Through mornings of chaos, and dinners a mess,
We manage to find the joy in the stress.
With silly selfies, we capture the glow,
Reflecting our hearts, just letting it flow.

So here's to the mirrors, and all that they hold,
The laughter, the love, the stories retold.
With every glance, we're wrapped up in cheer,
In this quirky reflection, forever we steer.

Whispers in the Wind

You dropped your socks, I found them here,
They smell like you, it's quite sincere.
A cuddly hug, a foot asleep,
Let's laugh so hard, our secrets keep.

Back to old tricks, coffee in bed,
You tell the jokes, I roll my head.
Your goofy dance, my sparkly glee,
At midnight snacks, it's you and me.

Rekindling the Light

A candle flickers, then goes out,
Your silly grin, it's what I shout.
Pasta on the walls, oh what a scene,
You lick your fingers, it's quite obscene.

Board games fail, we cheat and laugh,
You thank the cat for your autograph.
Finding the joy in simple things,
Like stealing fries and playful slings.

When Echoes Become Music

In the hallway, your voice sings,
I'm a butterfly, you're the wings.
Your tray of snacks, a feast divine,
You pour the soda, it's mostly mine.

Off-key singing in the shower,
Time stands still, what a power!
You trip, I catch you, what a sight,
Under the stars, we feel so light.

The Rebirth of Together

On the couch, we're piled high,
Old popcorn bags that never die.
Dance-offs in the kitchen late,
You step on toes; oh, isn't fate?

Hiccups loud, hilarious too,
You try to pout, I just see you.
With every jest, the laughter grows,
In our home, that warmth still glows.

Flames of Old

Once we were wild, like a bright spark,
Bumping and tussling till after dark.
Now after years, here we still snack,
Pillow fights bring back the old knack.

Remember that time we lost the cat?
You found it sleeping in your old hat.
With silly grins, we rolled on the floor,
Who knew chaos would lead us to more?

You burn the toast while I take a sip,
Yet from our mess, we still let it rip.
A dance in the kitchen, goofy and loud,
We set off the smoke alarm, feeling proud.

So let's build our fire with laughter anew,
The sparks of old can dance like they used to.
In this goofy game, we found the thrill,
With smiles and flares, we've had our fill.

A Symphony Replayed

You hit the wrong note; I laugh aloud,
Playing our song before the crowd.
With clanging pots and pans a-rattle,
The kitchen's a stage for our duet battle.

Remember the time you danced with a broom?
We twirled like stars in our tiny room.
Off-key harmonies fill up the night,
Yet somehow, darling, it all feels right.

You serenade me with laundry lines,
I join in with socks in different designs.
Our laughter echoes, a familiar score,
In this silly symphony, we long for more.

So let's hold hands and take a big bow,
Forget the rhythm; we'll wing it somehow.
With giggles and grins, we'll write our tune,
Together forever, like stars, we'll swoon.

Returns and Revelations

You stole my fries; was it really fair?
I let you know with a playful glare.
Yet here we are, laughing through the mess,
Discovering sparks in our mild excess.

Remember the time you forgot my birthday?
I made you pancakes in a funny way.
With whipped cream hats and silly grins,
We realized that fun is where it begins.

Chasing each other around the room,
Over old socks and that funky broom.
Revelations made as we share a pie,
The world's our stage, come let's give it a try!

So let's dive back into this old dance,
With every trip, we'll take a chance.
A waltz of giggles, in silly delight,
With every return, our hearts feel light.

The Tides of Us

Like waves crashing back, we're swept away,
With moments of laughter, we find our play.
Caught in the tide of our quirky dance,
Each twist and turn, another chance.

Remember the time we built that sand fort?
It crumbled down, but we just snorted.
With buckets of smiles and goofy grins,
Our tides of fun were where it begins.

Splashing through puddles and then a slip,
You fell in the mud, and I gave a tip.
Covered in dirt, we could barely stand,
Yet with giggles and joy, we joined hand in hand.

So let's ride the waves like a boat set free,
Navigating storms in our silly spree.
With every high tide, we'll soar above,
In this ocean of chaos, we found our love.

Timeless Affections

In a world of mismatched socks,
We stumble over quirky blocks.
Old photos make us giggle loud,
Rehashing tales beneath the crowd.

You spilled your drink, I lost my cool,
Yet here we are, two lovesick fools.
With laughter echoing in the air,
We chase our dreams with silly flair.

Each wink a spark, ignites the scene,
Like my spaghetti – saucy and keen.
Your snorts of joy, a sweet delight,
Together we shine, brilliant and bright.

So here's to quirks and silly charms,
In this crazy dance, we're still in arms.
With every twist, our hearts align,
In this timeless mess, forever mine.

Holding on to Yesterday

Remember the time you slipped on ice?
You laughed so hard, it was quite a slice.
A face full of snow, boots all askew,
I fell right after, trying to help you.

Old cassette tapes, we sang off-key,
Dancing like fools, just you and me.
Your awkward moves, they leave me weak,
As we bust a groove, strange as a peak.

When the phone rings, it's often a joke,
I'm still your clown, you're still my smoke.
We share our food, despite the fight,
You tried my fries, I took your bite.

Holding on tight to the days gone past,
In this sitcom of ours, we're unsurpassed.
With each passing chuckle, we just can't stray,
Here's to tomorrow: let's play all day!

Illuminated by Memory

Got a light? Oh wait, it's your smile,
Shining so bright, it's been a while!
We stumbled on memories, so bizarre,
Like that one time we rode a car.

Through twisted tales of playful cheating,
With pretzels and drinks, there's no defeating.
Each glance is a spark, igniting our spree,
As we whirl around in pure glee.

Unpredictable chaos in every stride,
Your quirky face I cannot bide.
From silly names to laughter in spades,
You're the sunshine that never fades.

So let's jump through puddles and wave at the moon,
With every heartbeat, we'll sing our tune.
In this dancehall of memories old,
We'll laugh for an eternity – brave and bold!

The Resurgence of Us

We found an old map, treasure assumed,
As usual, my sense of direction was doomed.
You laughed at my hatred for getting lost,
We made a pact, no matter the cost.

Through twist and turns, we rediscover,
Each squabble a game, another cover.
Like discovering snacks hidden in jars,
Our sweetness melts, no need for a spar.

On a blanket of stars, we lay side by side,
Recalling the days when we both cried.
Through every stumble, we laughed it away,
In the dance of our lives, solidly we sway.

So bring out the glitter and sparkles anew,
In this playful tale, it's just me and you.
With every slip, every silly thrust,
We rise from the ashes, a glorious gust.

The Return of Radiant Flames

Once were embers, now a blaze,
With silly jokes that last for days.
We dance like fools without a care,
Who knew we'd spark this wild affair?

Old flannel shirts, they're back in style,
The way you grin makes it all worthwhile.
We roast the marshmallows, make a mess,
Your smirk, my favorite kind of stress.

Your quirky laugh ignites my heart,
Our playful banter, a work of art.
Like puppy dogs, we chase the night,
With every giggle, we feel so light.

Between the flames and s'mores we find,
The joy that sparks once more defined.
In this silly dance of ours, we know,
We're two comedians stealing the show.

Resurgence of a Faded Touch

Forgotten kisses, now a tease,
You tickle my arm, oh please!
Your fingertips are back on track,
With every touch, I just fall back.

The socks you wear still mismatch too,
A charming style, just me and you.
With every wink, the past takes flight,
I never thought we'd feel this right.

Giggling at your old dad jokes,
We make each other howl like folks.
With silly puns, we play all night,
In your embrace, it feels so right.

Misplaced hats and crooked ties,
Your goofy grin still hypnotize.
In this joyride of twists and turns,
Our hearts collide, and passion burns.

Threads of Passion Woven Anew

Like knitting mishaps in a storm,
We stitch together, feeling warm.
Old patterns fade, but bright threads show,
How weaving hearts can make us glow.

Mistaken dishes in our feast,
You've burned the toast, it's quite the beast!
But laughter echoes in the room,
With every misstep, we find our bloom.

Sock puppets dance upon the floor,
With every giggle, we crave for more.
We trade off glances, sly and sweet,
Our yarn of joy is still complete.

In our cozy little blend,
We find the sparks that never end.
With every thread that we entwine,
We craft a love that's simply divine.

Soft Glances Across the Room

In crowded spaces, eyes collide,
A wink from you, I'm filled with pride.
The cheeky smiles that we've perfected,
In every glance, we feel connected.

You make a face while eating cake,
Your silly antics cause a quake.
With every nibble, laughter flows,
Our bond gets stronger, that's how it goes.

Amidst the chatter, soft and sweet,
We sneak a look, 'tis pure retreat.
In silent language, sparks are made,
With playful stares, our hearts invade.

Across the room, the magic brews,
With quirks and laughter, we can't lose.
In every moment, wild and free,
We cherish this sweet jubilee.

Echoes of You

I found a note from you today,
It said you'd steal my socks to play.
A love that's silly, bright as day,
With every laugh, you make me sway.

The coffee spills, the cat's a mess,
We joke about our weird excess.
You claim my snacks, I must confess,
With every bite, my heart's in bliss.

We're just two kids in grown-up suits,
Engaging in our funny hoots.
Circus tricks and silly toots,
Our hearts still dance in goofy boots.

So here we are, just you and me,
In our own bustling comedy.
Each silly giggle sets us free,
Your laughter's all my heart can see.

The Reunion of Souls

We met again at the old cafe,
You spilled your drink in such a way.
I laughed so hard, I lost my tray,
What a ridiculous display!

You showed up dressed in polka dots,
I still can't believe those silly thoughts.
We reminisce about the knots,
In our past loves and tangled plots.

Remember when you danced with flair?
Your moves, they made me stop and stare.
We swapped our jokes without a care,
Old friends and lovers on a dare.

Now we share our sweetest quirks,
Twirling 'round like silly jerks.
In every smile, our joy works,
In this reunion, love still lurks.

Shadows of Longing

The shadows dance when you are near,
They giggle softly, full of cheer.
We whisper secrets, laugh, my dear,
In this dim glow, our hearts reappear.

With playful nudges and silly sneezes,
Our hearts ignite, just like the breezes.
In silly games, our laughter pleases,
Time melts away, it never ceases.

Just look at us, what a sight to see,
Two old fools in perfect harmony.
We flirt with shadows, wild and free,
In this dance of ours, just you and me.

Throwing popcorn, counting clouds,
Our playful antics draw in crowds.
Surrounded by our laughter loud,
In love's soft glow, we're truly proud.

Softly Through the Mist

Through morning fog, I see your face,
In every giggle, I find my place.
With silly jokes, we share the space,
As misty thoughts drift and embrace.

Remember our dance, so out of tune?
You tripped and laughed beneath the moon.
In every blunder, our hearts attune,
With every flub, our joy's in bloom.

The wind plays tricks, you're such a tease,
You steal my hat just to appease.
In our own world, we do as we please,
Like two wild kids dancing with ease.

So here we stand, amidst the fight,
Our hearts are full, everything's right.
With each chuckle, we soar in flight,
Together, we banish all the night.

The Flame That Flickers

When we met, sparks flew, loud and bright,
Now we play tag in the dead of night.
Your socks on the floor, a peculiar sight,
But I still adore your giggles, quite the delight.

Old jokes get funnier with every retell,
Like your dance moves, needs a warning bell.
Our kitchen experiments? Oh what the smell!
Yet in all this chaos, I know it's swell.

We prattle like kids when the sun goes down,
Your puns are dreadful, yet I wear a crown.
With each playful jab, banter takes the town,
You're my favorite clown, in mismatched gown.

So let's pour some tea and laugh 'til we cry,
In this circus of ours, you are my pie.
With each silly moment, we'll tell time to fly,
Together forever, oh me, oh my!

Finding Home Again

Your hair's a mess, but it's still quite glam,
You lost the car keys? Oh, that's my jam!
We make a good team with toast and jam,
Who knew we'd end up like this, what a slam!

We squabble like siblings over cookie dough,
And wear each other's clothes, just for show.
With socks that clash and a unique glow,
We find the path where silly hearts flow.

In crowded malls with our shopping spree,
Navigating aisles became our decree.
Your loud laugh echoes, like waves from the sea,
I can't help but smile, oh what fun to be free!

So let's steal some chips, and make some new vows,
For moments like these, I could take a bow.
Here's to our home, where the laughter allows,
In this crazy love, we'll always endow.

Beneath the Autumn Sky

Under the trees, your hat flies away,
I chase it in circles, both cheeky and play.
You laugh till you cry, what a glorious day,
With leaves as our confetti, we dance and sway.

Pumpkin spice lattes, oh what a treat!
We lounge on the grass, feeling quite the feat.
You spill yours on me, oh that's hard to beat!
But in this mess, I find you so sweet.

Squirrels plotting theft of our picnic spread,
As we swat and shout, it's all in good tread.
With every mishap, new memories are bred,
Under autumn's smile, we're happily led.

So here's to the moments, wild and quite free,
Our autumn adventures, just you and me.
With laughter our guide, forever we'll be,
Painting our love, as bright as a tree.

Second Chances in Bloom

You forgot my birthday, let's not make a scene,
But that cake you made? Was it meant to be green?
We'll laugh it off, this quirky routine,
In our garden of goof, we reign supreme.

We plant new seeds, though they sprout with a twist,
Our uproarious efforts are hard to resist.
You say, "That's a flower," while I raise a fist,
Yet every misstep gets a chuckle, not missed.

With watering cans and mismatched gloves,
We argue like kids while the universe shoves.
In each playful banter, our friendship just loves,
Growing vibrant and wild, like beautiful doves.

So here's to the chaos, our quirky bouquet,
In laughter, we'll find our own silly way.
With blooms of absurdity, come what may,
Together forever, let's brighten the day!

Once More with Feeling

A second glance at tangled hair,
You spilled your coffee, I pretended to care.
I tripped on my own shoe, what a sight,
You laughed so hard, I felt alright.

Remember that time you danced on the floor?
Twinkle-toes, nearly knocked down a door!
With each silly mishap, hearts were on fire,
With giggles and snorts, we rose even higher.

We cracked a joke, then both lost our breath,
'You call that a look?' I questioned your heft.
A playful tease, my heart skipped a beat,
Two clowns together, oh, life is sweet!

So here's to those slips, the blunders we've made,
In a wacky romance, we've truly stayed.
With laughter as our glue, forever we'll play,
Each quirky moment, the best kind of day.

Threads of Yesterday

We found an old photo, what a delight,
You with a haircut that gave me a fright!
Those bell-bottoms swayed like a fish on a hook,
I couldn't help laughing, it's worth a look.

The ancient texts of our poetry gone,
You penned sweet verses, but forgot half the dawn.
Your rhymes had a rhythm, like a cat with a shoe,
My heart still dances to the sound of your cue.

We strolled through the park, our youth in tow,
You tried to impress with your karaoke show.
The notes strayed far, like a dog on a chase,
Yet in every screech, I found your sweet grace.

So let's stitch our past with a needle of light,
Crafting new memories, holding on tight.
With laughter as thread, we weave through the days,
In the dance of our mishaps, forever we'll blaze.

The Garden of Us

In the garden of dreams, where mishaps do bloom,
You watered the daisies, I filled up the room.
A sprinkler explosion, oh what a spray!
We giggled and danced in a floral ballet.

Picking ripe laughter from branches so high,
We planted our gags and watched them all fly.
Your veggie puns sprouted with every green twist,
Like flowers in spring, they simply can't miss.

While pruning the hedges, you fumbled a bee,
I dodged and I ducked, it's a sight to see!
With cherry tomatoes raining down from the sky,
We rolled on the grass, with tears in our eye.

As seasons do change, our garden will grow,
With laughter as fertilizer, happiness flows.
In the sun or the shade, our hearts stay robust,
In the garden of us, we thrive, there's no rust.

Sweet Nostalgia

Dusting off memories, they spring into view,
That time you wore socks with polka dots too!
You danced with a broom, I just laughed and we cried,
With every misstep, we enjoyed the wild ride.

The board games we played, you lost with a grin,
You plotted revenge, but I let the fun win.
Each roll of the dice brought chaos and cheer,
In the sweet slapstick, our hearts drew near.

Recalling the jokes, the goofy retorts,
You dressed as a pirate, I wore legal shorts.
With laughter our treasure, we sailed through the night,
Two swashbuckling mates, oh, what a delight!

So let's toast to the moments that sparkle and shine,
To the episodes past that blend yours and mine.
In the sweet mix of laughter and sappy old tales,
We found our forever, where nostalgia prevails.

Incandescent Moments Revisited

In the kitchen, sparks do fly,
As I attempt a pie.
Flour clouds and rolling pins,
Who knew cooking had so many sins?

Your laugh fills up the air,
Like burnt toast without a care.
Each mishap makes me grin,
Guess love is where the fun begins.

On the couch, we take a seat,
Fighting for the last sweet treat.
You claim it's my turn to share,
But I suspect, you're quite aware.

As we chuckle, hearts entwine,
In the chaos, we both shine.
Through silly games, we find our way,
Incandescent moments, come what may.

The Poetry of Us Rewritten

In the park, we play a game,
Who can shout the silliest name?
Giggling like children, side by side,
In this joy, we always confide.

Your puns are like a rhythmic dance,
My rolling eyes give them a chance.
Each quip is met with laughter loud,
A little silly, makes us proud.

Whenever you trip, it's all too bright,
Gravity seems to know our light.
With every stumble, my heart takes flight,
Two comic souls, oh what a sight!

So here's to us, in humorous views,
Rewriting stories we get to choose.
With every joke, you steal my breath,
In our own sonnet, we'll dance 'til death.

Whispers of the Past

Remember when we lost the keys?
We laughed so hard, fell to our knees.
Searching high and searching low,
Turns out, they were under your toe!

In old photos, our hair was wild,
You said I looked like a crazy child.
With silly grins, and outfits bold,
Oh how those memories never grow old.

We reminisce about our first date,
You spilled your drink, it was fate.
Covered in soda, you stole the show,
Romance blooms where laughter flows.

The whispers of days gone past,
Make our hearts beat unsurpassed.
In every giggle, the spark remains,
Through every joke, love entertains.

Embered Hearts Awaken

On a cold night, we start a fire,
You try to light it with sheer desire.
With sticks and rocks, you persevere,
A roaring flame brings you near.

S'mores and laughter fill the space,
Chocolate smudges on your face.
I laugh out loud, it's quite a sight,
Your marshmallow skills need more light!

With cuddles sweet and playful tease,
We toss blankets like a breeze.
In our fortress made of dreams,
Embered hearts glow, or so it seems.

So here's to moments, bright and bold,
Where warmth and laughter never grow old.
In our cozy haven, side by side,
Together forever, we'll abide.

Embracing the Past

Remembering the days gone by,
With awkward dances, oh my,
You tripped and fell right on your face,
I laughed so hard, had to leave the place.

But years have passed, we've found our groove,
Your silly moves still make me move,
We wear our quirks like a badge of pride,
In this strange love, we can't collide.

From thrift shop finds to goofy ties,
We share the laughs with no goodbyes,
Each silly joke a gentle tease,
You make me chuckle and feel at ease.

Together we'll dance through thick and thin,
With every stumble, let the fun begin,
Our love's a circus, a playful act,
In each moment, there's quirky impact.

Reawakening the Heart

You looked at me with that silly grin,
It made my head start to spin,
I thought of all our dated dates,
Those awkward laughs that changed our fates.

We caught our laughter like it was a game,
Each silly blunder igniting the flame,
With every quirk that made us blush,
You made my heartbeat race and rush.

In your old socks and mismatched shoes,
You dance like no one has any clues,
I'll trip with you; it's part of the plot,
In this wild rom-com, you're my favorite shot.

When you crack a joke and roll your eyes,
The world feels right, the sun will rise,
So here we are, just you and me,
With laughter galore, wild and free.

Starlit Memories

Under the moon, we laugh and sigh,
With jellybeans flying up to the sky,
You hiccuped once, then twice in a row,
Left me in stitches, oh what a show!

With old records spinning some tunes so sweet,
Your goofy dance moves—I admit they're neat,
A whirlwind of memories, both old and new,
Each silly moment—I adore them, too!

We've spun through mischief, each grin a spark,
Chasing fireflies 'til the light fades to dark,
The stars twinkle down at our clumsy feet,
In this awkward ballet, our hearts skip a beat.

So let's make more memories, oh groove with me,
With every laugh shared, wild and free,
Through starlit nights of laughter and cheer,
Your crazy antics, forever held dear.

In the Warmth of Your Embrace

Here we are wrapped in a quirky hug,
Your funny face gives me the warmest snug,
With spaghetti noodles tangled in hair,
We laugh out loud; it's love beyond compare!

You take my hand and then misstep,
Fall on the floor, oh what a prep,
We take the plunge and roll around,
With each laugh shared, we can't be drowned.

Let's twirl like clowns in an old parade,
Our laughter echoes, never to fade,
Each gentle squeeze feels like a jest,
In this weird duet, we know we're blessed.

With every tickle and gentle tease,
This funny dance brings us to our knees,
So hold me tight, let the giggles resound,
In the warmth of each embrace, joy is found.

The Unraveling of Winter's Chill

In the frost of a morning bright,
You slipped on ice, oh what a sight!
With a giggle that peeled the snow,
Warmth bloomed from a winter's glow.

Laughter danced in the chilly air,
You called me clumsy, made me stare.
But with each slip and fall we took,
We wrote new chapters in our book.

The coffee brews were far too hot,
You spilled some on the seat I sought.
Yet all I felt was pure delight,
In our tangled, playful winter fight.

Winter's chill began to sway,
As we both laughed our cares away.
In the warmth of laughter's play,
Our hearts bloomed in the sunny ray.

Stoking the Forgotten Fire

In the kitchen, pots began to bang,
You tried to dance, but it was more of a clang.
The recipe called for spice, not flair,
But we laughed so hard, we lit the air.

Like an old song on a classic beat,
Our hands fumbled; oh, but what a treat!
The smoke alarm sang a joyful tune,
As we hit the roof, just like a cartoon.

In a whirl of chaos, we found our groove,
With playful jabs and a goofy move.
Who knew a burnt dish could spark the light,
Of two old hearts, igniting the night?

As the flames flickered and stories soared,
Every laugh struck like sweet accord.
From ashes of the past, sparks twined,
In the kitchen, new sparks aligned.

A Second Chance Under Moonlight

Under the stars, we sat with snacks,
You tossed a chip, it hit my back!
With giggles echoing through the night,
We shared our dreams, under soft moonlight.

The breeze whispered secrets of old,
As we unfolded tales, both shy and bold.
You made a face, pretended to snore,
And our shared laughter opened the door.

A firefly buzzed, made us both jump,
You called it a robot – oh, such a plump!
With silly antics and jabbering chat,
We stitched our hearts on a lawn chair mat.

In this moment, no past to briar,
Just sparks flying, a renewed desire.
In the soft glow of our midnight scheme,
A second chance became a dream.

The Reunion of Lost Souls

In a café where the espresso brews,
You spilled it on my favorite shoes!
With laughter ringing 'round the place,
We both wore smiles, and a blush on our face.

The waiter rolled his eyes, what a scene,
As we joked like kids, feeling so keen.
A flick of your wrist, the sugar flew,
And once again, I was lost in you.

Oh, the menu had no hint of the past,
But in your eyes, the shadows were cast.
We shared old stories, in between bites,
And rekindled the spark of the delicious nights.

With every sip and playful tease,
We toasted to old cracks that were sure to please.
In the reunion of our silly souls,
We found our path, now patched with goals.

Serendipity's Embrace

In a café, we spill our tea,
Your laugh makes the waiter flee.
Silly glances fill the air,
As we dance on a single chair.

Forgotten notes in pockets deep,
We giggle at promises we couldn't keep.
Your hair's a mess, mine's the same,
Yet here we are, still playing the game.

With awkward hugs and playful shoves,
We navigate through our silly loves.
A toast to fate, with cups held high,
Who knew old flames would never die?

So here's to moments filled with cheer,
When serendipity draws us near.
In laughter's grip, we'll always stay,
Embracing joy in a quirky way.

Light After Dusk

In the glow of dimmed street lights,
You trip over your shoelace, oh what sights!
We share a chuckle, a gentle tease,
As we chase the shadows with comic ease.

Remember the days in silly hats?
You thought you could charm me with fancy chats.
With each clumsy step we take tonight,
We find the spark, it feels so right.

Under the stars, we reminisce,
Each moment a funny little bliss.
Your goofy grin brings warmth anew,
It's in these quirks I'm drawn to you.

As laughter bubbles up like fizz,
In this dance of joy, we find our whiz.
So here we stand, hearts in the dusk,
With playful banter, we shall trust.

Echoes of an Old Melody

A song plays softly, we hum along,
Off-key notes make our hearts feel strong.
Dance like no one's watching us,
As old memories turn to dust.

You misstep and almost fall,
But then you catch me, after all.
With laughter ringing in the air,
We twirl like kids without a care.

Your goofy grin brings memories back,
Of silly pranks and laughter's knack.
As echoes sway, we spin around,
In the rhythm of the love we found.

Hum along, you silly muse,
In our hearts, we can't lose.
With every note, a spark ignites,
In this dance, we shine so bright.

The Return of Color

Gray clouds parted, we broke the mold,
With vibrant hues of stories told.
Your mismatched socks, they make me grin,
In this colorful chaos, where we begin.

We paint the town with goofy signs,
Scribbles of hearts intertwined.
With splashes bright, we'll make it fun,
Old is new, and we've just begun.

In playful chaos, we spark our flare,
Through silly moments, we become a pair.
As puddles form from all our glee,
We jump right in, you and me.

Life's a canvas, let's make it wild,
With laughter's brush, we're reconciled.
Hand in hand, we'll take our chance,
In colors bright, we'll always dance.

A Dance of Forgotten Dreams

In the attic, dusty clothes,
We found an old pair of shoes.
They danced to tunes we forgot,
Two left feet, what a funny plot!

The old records played our song,
We laughed at how we got it wrong.
We twirled, we swayed, then tripped with flair,
It seems we still make quite the pair.

The walls echoed with our giggles,
Patchwork memories made us wiggle.
With every clash, we shared a smile,
Turns out we're still quite the wild style.

A dance of dreams, now stripped of dust,
Reminders of what was a must.
In twirls and spins, we found our way,
To love's encore, let's dance today!

The Heart's Gentle Resurgence

I found your sock under the bed,
Who knew it held neglected threads?
With every wash, it multiplies,
Guess it's not just us who tries.

Your old jokes still have that zest,
Even if they fail the test.
A pun-filled chat, we rehearse,
Each laughter like a little verse.

We baked a cake that turned to goo,
But who needs sweets when I've got you?
We grin and bear the mess we make,
Our hearts are light, for laughter's sake.

In cozy corners, we reminisce,
Forgotten moments now bring bliss.
With silly smiles and eyes that gleam,
We spark again our foolish dream.

Tapestry of Time

Your hair turned grey, but so has mine,
Like tangled threads, we've crossed the line.
Each laugh line tells of days gone by,
A tapestry we weave, oh my!

We tried to knit, but stuck the yarn,
A colorful mess, but it's our charm.
Still drafting patterns, bold and bright,
Knots of joy in the morning light.

We hang our memories on the wall,
A crooked frame, though we stand tall.
With every tale, we lose the frown,
Two quirky souls, still going round.

In this patchwork quilt, we find our way,
Through funky colors of every day.
Though threads may fray and sometimes bind,
It's you and me, intertwined.

Rewriting Our Story

Our first date still makes me sweat,
You spilled your drink, I'll never forget.
We laughed it off, then shared a fry,
Funny how time just seems to fly.

With every page, our plot unfolds,
A comedic twist, if truth be told.
We rewrote lines, and added spins,
Chapter by chapter, here our fun begins.

The plot thickened with each small blunder,
We turned our missteps into thunder.
With quirky lines and lots of cheer,
We painted tales that keep us near.

In this storybook of silly schemes,
We live in laughter, chase our dreams.
As we rewrite, let's take a chance,
On this wild ride of a second dance!

New Dawn

The coffee's brewing, a joyful sight,
You stole the blanket, oh what a fight!
Your morning breath, a fragrant delight,
Yet here we are, laughing in the light.

We dance to tunes of an old offbeat,
Each step a mishap, yet oh so sweet.
Stumbling together, our hearts take flight,
Who knew being goofy could feel so right?

We share our quirks like a prized collection,
You hide my keys—what a grand deception!
Yet in your eyes, there's so much reflection,
A world of silly, pure affection.

So here's to mornings, where laughter reigns,
And silly moments wash away the pains.
With every sunrise, our routines exchange,
Each day feels brand new, yet sweetly strange.

Old Flame

You tease me often, a playful game,
Like poking at embers to fan the flame.
Your silly puns always drive me insane,
Yet in this chaos, we both stake our claim.

A pizza date that ended in cheese,
You dropped it first, oh, such a tease!
We laugh and argue, never at ease,
But every moment brings us to our knees.

Misplaced your phone? Blame it on me!
I'll steal your fries, oh, can't you see?
Through goofy antics, we set our glee,
In this mixed-up dance, we just want to be.

So let's keep sparking this fun little quirk,
With silly tales and laughter, we'll not shirk.
An old flame's warmth still has its perk,
In humor we thrive, with no need to lurk.

The Pulse of Familiarity

You snore like a bear, and I'll never lie,
Yet every night, I smile with a sigh.
We've counted the stars, watched the clouds fly,
In this cozy chaos, my heart won't deny.

You hide my snacks, that old trick of yours,
In this sweet playful war, love always ensures.
Amidst all the chuckles, our connection restores,
In the rhythm of laughter, our hearts open doors.

Through inside jokes that only we get,
Our silly memories, how could I forget?
You're my partner in crime, the best kind of pet,
With you by my side, I'm forever in debt.

So here's to the quirks that make us unique,
In laughter we find what we both seek.
With every silly moment, our hearts tweak,
In this dance of familiarity, we're never weak.

Heartstrings Rewoven

Your sock on my chair, what a bold move!
In the symphony of us, you've found your groove.
We play the same song, never miss a beat,
Each note a reminder, your presence is sweet.

We bicker like siblings, but always with flair,
You know every flaw, yet don't even care.
Through laughter and squabbles, we weave our affair,
Each thread comes together, a tapestry rare.

In the whirlwind of life, you dance like no other,
Who else would dare to call me a smother?
With jokes like confetti that light up our path,
We stumble and grin, doing simple math.

So here's to the moments that tickle our hearts,
In this playful ballet, each day intertwines parts.
Through ups and downs, our comedic sparks,
Make this journey together, where joy never departs.

Flickers of Yesterday

Remember that time you wore polka dots?
I laughed so hard, I forgot all my thoughts.
Yet in our goofy moments, how time just rots,
Flickers of yesterday, sweet life's little knots.

We've danced in the kitchen, spilled flour galore,
Baked a soft cake that fell straight to the floor.
Yet in all the blunders that we both explore,
It's the laughter that lingers, forever encore.

Grazing through memories, sparks start to fly,
With every silly venture, we reach for the sky.
In the mix of our antics, we twinkle and sigh,
A heart full of warmth, oh my, how time flies.

So let's keep igniting those charming glows,
With a wink and a grin, our story still grows.
Each humorous bump just lovingly shows,
In the dance of our lives, how the joy overflows.

A Journey Back to You

Our paths once crossed, a dance so strange,
With mismatched socks and a big hair change.
You tripped on words, I fell on my feet,
Yet here we are, still laughing, sweet.

We lost our way on that silly road,
Who knew the map was a joke bestowed?
But like two magnets, we spark and collide,
Through all the chaos, you're my goofy guide.

Remember the time, we tried to cook?
Flames on the stove, what a funny nook!
Yet through the smoke, your smile stayed bright,
In the ashes of laughter, everything's right.

So here we tread, back to our muse,
With rubber chickens and worn-out shoes.
The journey is silly, but oh so true,
I can't help but smile while I'm back with you.

Unfolding a Timeworn Tale

In dusty corners, our stories sleep,
With loads of giggles, a treasure deep.
We fought with pillows, staged a big show,
Like clowns in love, oh how we glow!

Your coffee spill made my heart take flight,
Like cartoon hearts, floating in the night.
Old records play that familiar tune,
As we whirl around like a couple of loons.

We found old letters, with doodles so bright,
A map to adventures on a starry night.
Your goofy grin, a spark in my chest,
Each moment with you, I must confess, I'm blessed.

So turn the pages, let's laugh with glee,
This ancient saga is crazy and free.
Together we skitter, like kids in the sun,
Unfolding the tale, oh what fun we've begun!

The Palette of Reimagined Dreams

We paint our days in colors untrue,
With splashes of chaos, oh what a view!
Your purple socks and my polka-dot tie,
Joke's on the canvas, we both know why.

Neon pink hearts float above our heads,
While we trip over all the paint-splattered threads.
Every brushstroke a giggle, a sigh,
As we create our masterpiece on the fly.

Your laughter is sunlight, fuels every hue,
Mixing bright joy with a shade or two.
Let's dance on the palette, no need for a scheme,
In this zany art, we'll follow the dream.

So gather the colors, let's splash and twirl,
With paintbrushes flying, we'll give it a whirl.
In this painted world, you're my favorite scene,
Together we'll daub, with a laugh and a gleam.

Heartbeats in Harmonious Rhythm

Your snoring's a tune, a symphony sweet,
Like jazz in the night, keeping time on repeat.
We dance through the quirks, your shoes on my toes,
In this waltz of weird, our laughter just flows.

Two hearts in sync, but the beat's a bit off,
With silly missteps, a giggling scoff.
I step on your dreams, you trip on the rug,
Yet here we stay, wrapped in the hug.

Our rhythm a shuffle, a merry-go-round,
With every misbeat, there's joy to be found.
In this comedic ballet, we glide with ease,
Through the hum of our lives, we dance and we tease.

So here's to the clumsiness that makes us thrive,
Every odd moment keeps the spark alive.
With heartbeats in laughter, we'll dance through the night,

In our quirky duet, everything feels right.

When Paths Cross Again

Two lost shoes on a crowded street,
Left behind by a love that felt sweet.
We tripped over fate in the strangest way,
Laughter emerged, and here we stay.

Old jokes rekindle what once felt right,
As we dance around in the soft moonlight.
With a wink and a playful nudge,
We forgot all that hate and held a grudge.

Our favorite diner, we return on a whim,
With fries and shakes, let the old tales begin.
The waitress rolls her eyes, says, 'Oh no, not you!'
But she knows we bring chaos, and that's nothing new.

A surprise party for two, no one thought of us,
We show up late, stirring that old-fashioned fuss.
With every awkward moment, our spark's flown high,
Two lost souls reunited, oh me, oh my!

Between Pages of Time

Dusty tomes on a shelf so old,
We leaf through laughter, happily bold.
Stories forgotten, we giggle and sigh,
As we brush off the years, like glitter on pie.

Misprinted pages tell of our dreams,
In pencil and ink, our old, silly schemes.
Bookmarks with scribbles, we read with delight,
Every chapter a memory, makes everything bright.

In a plot twist, we find a lost rhyme,
In the margins, our hearts interwine.
With a wink and a grin, we pen a new tale,
In the library of laughter, we'll never fail.

So here's to the stories that never grow old,
In the spine of our friendship, warmth takes hold.
Between every page, we'll always remember,
The humor of life makes the heart burn like ember.

Rediscovering the Spark

In old comic strips, our laughs come alive,
As we reminisce about how we'd survive.
A game of charades in the kitchen at dusk,
Lobster thermidor? Nah, just old pizza crust!

We tried rekindling with a fancy first date,
But tripped over spaghetti, oh what a fate!
With sauce on the ceiling and laughter so loud,
We promised to always throw fun in the crowd.

Old mixtapes tucked in the back of the car,
With songs from the past, we've come quite far.
Using cassette players all out of style,
We jam in the driveway, you can't help but smile.

A whimsy dance in rain-soaked shoes,
Caught in the moment, we forget all our blues.
Rediscovering sparks in this chaotic swirl,
Two clumsy hearts take on the world.

The Softest Reminder

Cuddly old sweaters from years long gone,
Each thread tells a tale, where we once shone.
With a tug and a pull, they shrink and play,
A fashion disaster, but hey, that's okay!

Ice cream cone drips on the sidewalk sweet,
We chase after flavors, our hearts skip a beat.
Banana split laughs, sprinkled with glee,
Two scoops of chaos, I'm happy with thee.

Walks in the park where squirrels make mess,
They toss down their acorns, it's anyone's guess.
Laughter erupts as we dodge their spree,
Nature's reminder of our jubilee.

With every soft glance, there's a giggle inside,
Two hearts intertwined, oh how we collide!
In the simplest moments, joy finds its way,
A sprinkle of humor brightens our day.

Awash in Old Melodies

We danced in the kitchen, two left feet,
Spilled coffee while laughing, oh, what a treat.
Your socks mismatched, with flair, avant-garde,
A waltz of blunders, our future feels starred.

The radio crackles with tunes from our youth,
As we sing off-key, but it's all good truth.
I swear you stepped on the dog's fluffy tail,
He joins in our chorus, oh, life is a trail.

Through vinyl and chaos, our hearts stay in tune,
With awkward embraces under the full moon.
I trip on the rug, you catch me, oh dear,
With laughter and smiles, it's blissful right here.

In this melody whirl, we find our soft spot,
A jest and a jive, let's dance like it's not.
Our rhythm unique, no choreography planned,
In music and mishaps, forever we'll stand.

The Light That Leads Us Home

Back to the couch where the snacks always wait,
You stole my last chip, oh, isn't that great?
With popcorn and giggles, we binge on old shows,
In this cozy chaos, our silliness grows.

The light flicks on like our shared memory,
A glance, and we snicker, it's all meant to be.
The cat cleans his paws, judging our fun,
We call him our referee, under the sun.

With goofy recaps, who played that last part?
You crack me up still, you've stolen my heart.
Our evenings of laughter, a quirky duet,
In our little sitcom, there's no room for regret.

As sunsets paint skies in bold, loony hues,
We tickle each other, playfully muse.
With a wink and a grin, let's never say stop,
We'll cherish these moments, our laughter won't drop.

Cherished Companionship

We share this weird hat, you know, just for fun,
A fashion statement, two peas on the run.
With matching T-shirts, a sight to behold,
Our quirks painted brightly, we've broken the mold.

You quote silly movies; I roll my old eyes,
But you crack me up with your crazy wise lies.
In conversations that twist like our pasta at night,
We delve into banter, our spirits feel light.

Your snoring's an anthem, a lullaby sweet,
I pretend it's a concert, a hit on repeat.
With cuddly adventures, we roam side by side,
In this quirky journey, our joy is our guide.

Through tickles and teasing, our hearts lift and soar,
In the dance of companionship, I always want more.
So here's to our odyssey, both silly and grand,
Forever together, we'll take on this land.

Old Talismans and New Beginnings

Found your old sweater at the back of the drawer,
Sniffed it like treasure, oh, I want it more!
With long-ago scents that tickle and tease,
We laugh at the crumbs that dangle from cheese.

Your old cassette tapes are dusty, it's true,
But playing them now brings back the old you.
We groove to the tunes with a bump and a grind,
In the rhythm of laughter, new memories unwind.

Those goofy old photos, our hair gone astray,
Can't help but chuckle, we've aged in a way.
Still, our hearts stay as young as the bright autumn leaves,
In this curious dance, joy is what we weave.

So here's to the artifacts of our past embrace,
A treasure trove shared, each giggle a trace.
With old talismans found and new laughs to enjoy,
Together forever, oh, how we've found joy!

Tides of Familiarity

We met again in a busy café,
Your latte art made my day.
You spilled the milk all on your sleeve,
I laughed so hard, I couldn't believe.

Old jokes came back like a friendly ghost,
You mentioned those cats we used to host.
With every sip, new tales emerged,
Like old ships sailing, our hearts surged.

We danced between the tables, so bold,
With every laugh, the warmth did unfold.
Your sneaky wink, a mischievous hint,
In this whirlwind, I can't help but sprint.

Oh, the tales that we once had spun,
Now come alive, oh what fun!
Familiar tides, they wash ashore,
In every drop, I love you more!

Serendipity in Bloom

Running into you at the flower stand,
A bouquet in my hand, almost planned.
You sneezed so loud, it startled the blooms,
Today, I swear, they danced in the rooms.

We picked daisies, laughing at their fate,
You wore a crown, oh, wasn't it great?
Your goofy grin, like a sunbeam's glow,
In this garden, we both overflowed.

Petals drifting in the afternoon light,
We chased them down, what a funny sight.
Clumsy and wild, we tangled our threads,
With every chuckle, we dropped our dread.

So here we stand, in serendipity's game,
Each moment shared, never the same.
Flowers bloom, and so do we,
In this silly dance, you're still my glee.

When Time Stood Still Again

In a moment caught in a quirky freeze,
You tripped on air, oh, such a tease!
We laughed at clocks that couldn't tick,
Time unraveled fast, like magic sticks.

Your hair a mess from the wild breeze,
Yet in my heart, it's pure expertise.
You winked at me with that cheeky flair,
Like we were kids, without a care.

We tossed our worries like paper planes,
Full of dreams, in sunlight's reigns.
As seconds trickled in our jest,
This silly pause felt like our best.

In time's embrace, we danced so sly,
Two silly souls beneath the sky.
When all stood still, we found our groove,
In this funny twist, I just can't move.

Hearts Rewritten in Starlight

Under the stars, we made a bet,
To twirl like sprites, no regret.
You stepped on my toes and laughed so loud,
Our clumsy rhythm drew quite a crowd.

With every fumble, sparks would fly,
We traded glances like clouds in the sky.
You stole my fries, I stole your drink,
In this silly mess, we didn't think.

The night was young, and so were we,
In every chuckle, we felt so free.
With starlit giggles that twinkled bright,
Our hearts rewrote the pages of night.

In this comedy, we took our stand,
With every move, we made our brand.
The cosmos danced to our quirky beat,
In this starry play, our hearts repeat.

Between the Lines of Silence

In quiet moments, we exchange a glance,
With just a look, we revive our dance.
You smirk at my socks, mismatched, it's true,
But I still wear them, they remind me of you.

The coffee's cold, but our jokes are warm,
We laugh at the chaos, it feels like a charm.
Forgotten dates, the times that we missed,
Yet here we are, back in the twist.

Like berries and cream, we mix and we blend,
A bit of the past, with a dash to extend.
You roll your eyes at my silly puns,
But your smile says it all, we're still number one.

Amongst all the noise, we find our tune,
Like two clowns in a circus, it feels so opportune.
In the space between, we do something right,
Who knew silence could spark such delight?

The Dance of Familiar Shadows

In the twilight glow, we trip on our feet,
Spinning in circles, you make laughter sweet.
Your shadow swings low, while I leap and twirl,
We dance like kids, as the stars start to whirl.

You poke at my knee with that playful grin,
Reminding me fondly, where we've been.
The echoes of giggles fill up the night,
As we stumble through memories, giggling in flight.

Your hair in the wind, it's a sight to behold,
As you juggle my snacks, never shy, never cold.
In tandem we share our quirky old ways,
Sprinkling our antics like confetti through days.

Under the moon, we forget what's ahead,
The past feels alive, no reason to dread.
With a wink and a nudge, we license this fun,
In the dance of our shadows, we're never done.

Threads of Yesterday's Embrace

Like patchwork quilts, our moments align,
Stitched with the laughter, they age like fine wine.
You pull at the threads, unravel my tease,
But I tie them back up with playful ease.

In the attic of time, we rummage for gold,
Finding treasure in stories cheerfully told.
Your face is a canvas, with brushstrokes of glee,
As we paint our adventures, just you and me.

We crack up at blunders, the fails of our youth,
While sipping on cider, we cherish the truth.
In tangled-up tales, we find joy in the mess,
Who knew nostalgia could feel like a caress?

With every patch added, we dance 'round the room,
Creating a tapestry, letting it bloom.
In every odd memory, we chuckle and sigh,
Threads woven with laughter — we'll always comply.

An Invitation to Walk Again

Let's wander the paths where we once lost track,
With popcorn in hand, and a wink, we'll unpack.
You'll trip on a pebble, I'll laugh at your style,
And sprinkle our stumbles with humor and guile.

The old tree swings low, still holding our names,
We'll jump in the leaves, like kids in our games.
With a toss of a branch, and a push from below,
We'll giggle and glide, like the river we flow.

A map of our memories, let's chart it anew,
Crossing off 'dare' to try 'tickle your shoe.'
As the sun sets low, we'll embrace the fun,
Like two silly ducks, who have finally run.

So grab my arm tight, let's venture once more,
Side by side, we'll push open that door.
With laughter as fuel, we'll wander and play,
In this charming revival, we'll brighten the day.

Indicators of the Heart

When you steal my fries, my heart does a dance,
Your goofy grin sparks a second chance.
We trade silly looks across the crowded room,
Like kids playing tag, we break all the gloom.

Your socks do not match, but who really cares?
With every clumsy step, our laughter flares.
We share the last cookie, it crumbles and flies,
In this sweet little chaos, our spark never dies.

Your jokes—oh so bad, they're perfectly timed,
In the symphony of chuckles, our hearts are rhymed.
We dance like two penguins, just having a ball,
In the circus of us, I'm having a ball.

So here's to those flops where we stumble and sway,
Every trip, every fall, keeps the boredom at bay.
With each silly moment, we find our own way,
In this beautiful mess, together we stay.

Moments Reimagined

You bring me my coffee, but it's salt instead,
I give you a wink, so you don't feel misled.
We giggle like children with secrets to share,
In the cluttered kitchen, we float without care.

When you wear my sweater, it's two sizes too big,
You twirl like a dancer, let's do a little jig.
Our mismatched reminders paint joy on the wall,
Every crooked picture feels like a ball.

You trip on your laces, I burst out in glee,
We share tongue-tied secrets like sipping sweet tea.
Each moment's a canvas—a laugh or a sigh,
With you at my side, I'm ready to fly.

So here's to the times that we've stumbled in fun,
Painting our lives under the same shining sun.
With humor and laughter and a wink just for you,
Let's reimagine moments, make them feel new.

The Fire Returns

Remember that time when we both lost the plot,
In the kitchen you spilled, oh my, what a lot!
Pasta on ceilings, sauce dripping like rain,
We laughed till we cried, through the sweet chaos gained.

Our movie nights were noisy, popcorn on fire,
Every mishap brought us two steps higher.
The cat, he was dancing, the dog stole the show,
In this circus of life, where did our worries go?

With every spilled drink and a pastry disaster,
You winked with a grin, made my heartbeat faster.
We fumbled through days like clumsy old pals,
And rekindle the spark with our giggling yowls.

So, let's light that fire with splashes of cheer,
Every jump scares our hearts, but I've got you near.
In this waltz of the wild, let's keep our hearts free,
With your goofy charm, it's the best place to be.

Breathing Life into Us

In the morning you snort as you sway out of bed,
I can't help but laugh at the thoughts in my head.
Your bedhead's a masterpiece—artistic, for sure,
In our sleepy delight, I can't help but adore.

We skip like two kids, chasing dreams in the park,
Our laughter, a symphony, brightening the dark.
Every silly pun is a stitch in our quilt,
In the fabric of joy, our hearts are both built.

The world feels kinder when you dance and you sway,
With my heart in your hands, laughing worries away.
You juggle those errands with grace and with flair,
Making mundane life feel like a grand Ferris Square.

So here's to the moments where laughter takes flight,
Breathing life into us, we'll soar into the night.
With each chuckle and grin, in your warmth, I am free,
In our wacky adventure, just you and me.

www.ingramcontent.com/pod-product-compliance
Ingram Content Group UK Ltd.
Pitfield, Milton Keynes, MK11 3LW, UK
UKHW021116181224
452675UK00023B/1603